PRAYER
Worrier

Turning Every *Worry* into Powerful Prayer

Jennifer Waddle

Noble Theme Press

Prayer Worrier: Turning Every Worry into Powerful Prayer

Dedication

In memory of my Grandma Helen, who taught me to pray.

Table of Contents

Introduction

My Grandma Helen was one of the most influential people in my life. She taught me how to cook, sew, pray, and...worry. I still remember her sitting in her favorite blue chair, whispering aloud the worries of her heart.

Now, whether I actually learned how to worry from my sweet grandma, I do not know. But what I do know is this: Worry became an unwanted companion that never left my side.

It determined whether I had a good day or bad day.

It governed most of my decisions.

It caused me to react instead of respond.

It caused sleep loss, weight gain, and other physical problems.

It began to hurt my relationships.

Most of all, worry stole my joy.

That unwanted companion became the one I automatically turned to in times of trouble. Instead of seeking God's comforting guidance, I sought worry as a way of coping. I fretted over insignificant things, obsessed over what-ifs, rehearsed worse-case scenarios in my mind, and eventually...I broke.

Can you relate?

If any of my words describe your life, take heart, my friend. There is a way to stop the worry cycle.

In this study, I'd like to show you how every one of your worries can be turned into powerful prayers. Not only that, I'd like to show you how to leave that unwanted companion behind and live the life of freedom Jesus promised.

I do have to warn you, though. This journey isn't going to be easy. Us "worriers" have become extremely dependent on our fretful thinking. However, I will share the steps I've taken and the breakthroughs I've experienced as I've learned how to identify worry quickly and turn it into powerful prayer.

The format of this book will allow you to read each chapter, ponder thought-provoking questions, journal your responses, and follow up with three days of devotions. I pray you will take a few minutes each day to get into the Scriptures and pray for wisdom. Most of all, I pray that God will begin to peel away the layers of worry and enable you to release them to Him.

At any point along the way, I want you to feel free to email me with questions, concerns, or prayer requests. I do my best to answer every email that lands in my inbox!

I am so very grateful to be on this journey with you. May the Lord bless us and keep us as we seek His comfort and presence in our lives, and turn every worry into powerful prayer.

Always an email away,

Jennifer

jennifer@encouragementmama.com

"Therefore I tell you, do not be anxious about
your life, what you will eat or what you will drink,
nor about your body, what you will put on.
Is not life more than food, and the body more
than clothing? Look at the birds of the air:
they neither sow nor reap nor gather into barns,
and yet your heavenly Father feeds them.
Are you not of more value than they?
And which of you by being anxious
can add a single hour to his span of life?"

~Matthew 6:25-27 ESV

Chapter One:

First Worries

Y ou may not remember the first time worry entered your life, or what caused your young heart to flutter with uncertainty. But I clearly remember one of my first moments of anxiety, and it has stuck with me all these years.

It was the time my little brother and I rode the Joy Bus.

The Joy Bus was a big, white bus that came through the neighborhoods to pick up kids for the Wednesday night service at one of the local churches. One evening, my mom decided to let me and my brother and go. Now, my brother was probably around two at the time, and I was five and a half. As a doting sister, I felt *very responsible* for my brother's safety. And the minute we got on that bus, I started to worry.

I sat my little brother right beside me and didn't let any of the rowdy kids near him. I looked out the window as the familiarity of my neighborhood led to an unfamiliar part of town. The leaders in the front of the bus began singing songs with us, and as a very musical child, I was happy at first. Then they got to a verse that said, *"If the devil doesn't like it he can sit on a tack, sit on a tack, sit on a tack..."*

I did NOT like the fact that they were singing about the devil!

I did not like them singing about sitting on a tack!

I suddenly didn't like the Joy Bus at all!

My worried little self became very anxious, and I couldn't wait for the song to be over. Once we got to the church, they lined us up according to age, and my brother was whisked away to the preschool room.

I cried.

I didn't know the people who were taking him, and I thought for sure they wouldn't care for him like I would. I fretted the entire time until we were finally taken home. And you know what? We never rode the Joy Bus again! I can laugh about it now, but it was one of the first times I was truly worried.

What about you? What are some of your first worries? Have any of those worries carried over into your adult life? Perhaps you can relate to one of these scenarios:

- You didn't feel protected as a child so now you overprotect your loved ones, sheltering them and passing your anxiety onto them.
- Your parents divorced when you were young, so you are constantly worried about your own marriage. You tend to be fearful and even a bit paranoid.
- One of your family members was frequently sick, so now you constantly worry about your own health and the health of your loved ones.
- You felt abandoned as a child and now you are overly worried about being abandoned again.
- You grew up without a lot of money, so now you constantly worry about not having enough.

Of course, these are only a sample of childhood worries that can carry over into our adult lives. I'm sure you could write your own worry scenario and connect the dots as to how you live your life today.

Now before you think I'm trying to turn this study into a form of psychoanalysis or something, please understand that is not my intention at all. My goal is simply to get us to recognize how our first worries may have become ingrained in us and formed an unwelcome worry habit. In order to live worry-less lives, we need to address some of the ways our childhood worries may be influencing our walk today.

> In order to live worry-less lives, we need to address some of the ways our childhood worries may be influencing our walk today.

For me, after I got married and had my first two sons, I became like that five-year-old girl on the Joy Bus again. I sheltered my boys, tried to keep rowdy children away, covered their ears against songs about the devil, and pretty much worried myself sick over them. From the time they woke up, to the time they were tucked in bed, I fretted over those boys until I almost went bonkers. Fortunately, the Lord was patient with me and slowly grew me into a much different mother after my daughter was born. It was actually during a time of extreme worry that I offered a simple yet powerful prayer that began to change everything. This is how it happened:

Our sweet Hannah was born with a full head of hair, rosy cheeks, and a cute little scowl. She was placed in my arms and I kissed her forehead, thanking God again and again for our girl. With two boys at home, we were thrilled to have a daughter!

Moments later, the nurse peered over my shoulder and immediately said, "I need to take her for a minute."

Before we knew it, more nurses were coming in, as well as doctors and other staff members. Something was blocking Hannah's airway and she was gasping for air. They suctioned and suctioned and finally rushed her to the NICU to be intubated. Of course, we were worried to death. My husband followed the nurses, trying to stay as close to our baby as possible.

When I was able, I went to the NICU to get an update. Seeing my newborn hooked up to all the tubes was horrible. I felt like I was in a dream—a very bad dream.

> Seeing my newborn hooked up to all those tubes was horrible. I felt like I was in a dream—a very bad dream.

The doctor on-call came over and ushered us to another room. He said there was a "mass" coming down from behind her soft pallet and was blocking her airway. He then said something that shocked us to the core. He said it was possible the bones at the bottom of her skull had not fused together and her brain was actually coming down—literally into her throat.

We were sick. We clung to each other, not having a clue what the next days would bring. The doctor left quickly, stating they would do a CT scan to determine what the mass really was. The next several hours were a blur. I was on my feet practically from the moment I delivered her. Weary and helpless, the news finally came.

It was not Hannah's brain that was coming down into her throat—it was a tumor. Fortunately, it was benign, but she would need to have major surgery. They immediately transported her to Denver Children's Hospital. We drove home to pack a bag and say goodbye to our boys. At five and six, they didn't understand what was happening to their tiny sister. I felt so torn between staying to comfort them and leaving to be with my baby.

The next day, we met the doctor who would be performing the surgery. She informed us that she had dealt with this kind of tumor before, but she warned us that it was in a very difficult spot. She went on to say that it was possible Hannah wouldn't be able to swallow or speak, and that there were definite risks from such an invasive surgery.

After the hours-long procedure, when I finally saw my girl, I couldn't help but cry. She was so pale and swollen, and her little tongue was hanging out of her mouth. She didn't even look like the same baby. It was awful.

It was during our time in the hospital that my faith in God was tested beyond anything I'd ever experienced. I sensed Him telling me that I would need to trust Him fully, even if He chose to take her to heaven.

The thought terrified me. It overwhelmed me. It made me want to beg and plead and cry. If I'm completely honest, it threatened my trust in a loving Creator.

> The thought that God might choose to take
> our baby threatened my trust in Him.

But God...

In God's great love, provision, and purpose, He brought me to a place where I was able to surrender my baby completely to Him. I remember leaning over the plastic bassinet with a broken heart and a cracked voice singing,

"God is so good, God is so good, God is so good, He's so good to me."

Over and over I sang that chorus. And each time, I believed it a little more than the time before.

Bit by bit, Hannah began to heal. She reached milestone after milestone, as we saw that she was able to swallow, make sounds, and hear. The nerves in her face were not damaged. And two weeks later, she went home to meet her older brothers.

Although worry had been a constant part of my life, through that experience, something in me broke. That desperate need to hold on to everyone, to keep them safe, and to prevent everything bad from happening was finally released into the hands of God with one simple phrase: God is so good.

> That desperate need to hold on to everyone,
> to keep them safe, and to prevent everything bad from
> happening, was finally released into the hands of God.

So, I ask you the difficult question: Can you honestly say, "No matter what, God is still good"?

Over the next several chapters, we will see how our deepest worries, our strongest fears, and our most persistent anxieties can be turned into powerful prayers that will rise like incense before the throne of God. And it begins with one sentence: God is so good.

Chapter One: Thoughts to Ponder and Questions to Discuss

What were some of your first worries as a child?

_____

_____

_____

_____

Is it possible some of your persistent worries have been carried over from your childhood? If so, try to identify some of them now.

_____

_____

_____

_____

It's important to reach a place where we can say, "God is good, no matter what." Have you ever been challenged with that kind of trust?

_____

_____

_____

_____

Please read James 1:2-8 and list the benefits of going through various trials.

_____

_____

_____

_____

Please read 2 Timothy 1:13-14. What words are we supposed to hold fast? By what power can we do that?

_____

_____

_____

_____

_____

Do you struggle with knowing that God hears you? How do you usually react when you think God is silent or uncaring? Please read 1 John 5:14-15. How should we ask God for things? Does this mean we will get everything we want?

_____

_____

_____

_____

_____

Write a prayer of surrender to God, offering past, present, and future worries to Him.

_____

_____

_____

_____

_____

_____

_____

_____

_____

_____

_____

_____

Powerful prayer to leave first worries behind:

Gracious God, You have been with us from the very first moment we were conceived in our mother's womb. You knit us together and breathed life into us. We are Yours. Please forgive us for lacking trust in You. As we faced many worries as children, Lord, we allowed some of them to carry over into our adult lives. We lay those first worries before You now. Help us to leave them behind today and be filled with a renewed sense of peace and trust. Thank You for hedging us in, behind and before. We have nothing to fear. You are a good, good Father, and we look to You to help us overcome persistent worry. In Jesus' name, amen.

Chapter One: Daily Devotions

Day One: Letting Go of First Worries

Scriptures: Please read Isaiah 43:1-2, 5-7.

The Lord's assurance to Israel was that He had formed them and created them. He redeemed them and called them by name. What other promises did God make in Isaiah 43:2?

_____

_____

_____

_____

Do you believe God's promises for your own life as well? Why or why not?

_____

_____

_____

_____

_____

Re-read Isaiah 43:7. Are you called by His Name? Were you created for God's glory? Declare your gratefulness in bearing the name of the Lord.

_____

_____

_____

_____

_____

Write a word of praise to God, thanking Him for redeeming your life from all past worries.

_____

_____

_____

_____

_____

_____

_____

Day Two: **Recognizing a Bad Habit**

Scriptures: Please read Psalm 1:1-3.

The Psalm says, "Blessed are those who do not...

walk _____

stand _____

sit _____

In what way can we find great delight?

_____

_____

What does it mean to meditate on the Word of God day and night?

_____

_____

_____

_____

How can meditating on truth replace the bad habit of worry?

_____

_____

_____

_____

List a worry habit that is not beneficial. Be honest with God and yourself.

_____

_____

_____

Day Three: **He Hears**

Scriptures: Please read Psalm 4:1-8.

What assurance do we have from Psalm 4:3?

_____

_____

_____

Verses 4 & 5 encourage us to "be still and put our trust in the Lord." How difficult is it for you to be still in the midst of worry? What is your typical course of action?

_____

_____

_____

_____

Verses 7 & 8 contain the words *gladness, peace, rest, and safety.* What are the antonyms (opposites) of these words?

_____

_____

_____

_____

Notice how unresolved worry causes us to experience the opposite of the "light of God's countenance." How important is it to remove unresolved worry from our lives?

_____

_____

_____

_____

Write your own powerful prayer in letting go of past worries:

_____

_____

_____

_____

_____

_____

_____

_____

_____

_____

_____

_____

_____

_____

_____

Takeaway from Chapter One:

There is power in letting go of past worries and being
able to say, "God is good, no matter what."

Chapter Two:

The Lie That Worry Works

I used to buy into the idea that if I didn't worry, who would? I believed it was my *job* to worry. I thought that by worrying hard enough, it would either prevent something bad from happening or cause something good to happen. I even told my husband once that if he would worry a little more, I wouldn't have to!

What a terrible lie we have believed—the lie that worry works. You see, the enemy wants nothing more than for us to cling to anxious living. For he knows that when we are caught in that endless cycle of worry, we are not fully trusting God.

> The enemy wants nothing more than
> for us to cling to anxious living.

Remember what we discussed in the last chapter?

It's possible that we *learned* how to worry at a young age and allowed it to become a constant part of our lives. And now, we have to un-learn it.

One of the best ways to un-learn a habit is to replace it with a new, better one. And that new, better habit is God's truth.

"Fear not, for I am with you; be not dismayed, for I am your God. I will strengthen you, yes, I will help you, I will uphold you with My righteous right hand." (Isaiah 41:10)

"Rest in the Lord, and wait patiently for Him; do not fret because of him who prospers in his way, because of the man who brings wicked schemes to pass. Cease from anger, and forsake wrath; do not fret—it only causes harm." (Psalm 37:7-8)

Three times, in the first eight verses of Psalm 37, David says, "Do not fret." Fretting torments us. And the Bible says it only causes harm.

Yes, it is perfectly normal for us to be concerned about something or to contemplate how to solve a problem. After all, we have legitimate cares in this life. But when do our legitimate cares turn into a fretful, tormented state of mind?

Joanna Weaver, author of *Having a Mary Heart in a Martha World*, shares this:

> *"I come from a long line of Swedish worriers. 'Käre mej,' my Grandma Anna used to say over and over. 'Dear me, dear me.' Too high, too fast. Too much, too little.*
>
> *With all the potential danger in the world, there seemed to be only one response—worry. I remember lying in bed at night going over my list of fears. Somehow, as a young teenager, I had determined that the secret for avoiding trouble was to worry about it. In fact, I worried if I forgot to worry about something."*

<blockquote>
"I worried if I forgot
to worry about something."
~Joanna Weaver
</blockquote>

Can you relate to Joanna's words? Do you mistakenly believe that worrying about something will help you avoid trouble? (Weaver, Joanna *Having a Mary Heart in a Martha World: Finding Intimacy with God in the Busyness of Life*. United States: Waterbrook)

I can't tell you how many times fear and anxiety have stolen precious hours, days, and even months of my life. But when we allow the cares of the world to blow in from every direction—unfiltered and unchecked—we are really allowing winds of defeat to overcome us.

Think of it this way: If there was a storm outside with rain, lightning, and wind, we would close every window in the house, right? Why then do we let the showers of worry come in to saturate every thought?

Sisters, God is our refuge in times of trouble! In Him there is protection, shelter, and rest. Psalm 91 assures us of this:

> "He who dwells in the shelter of the Most High will rest in the shadow of the Almighty. I will say of the Lord, He is my refuge and my fortress, my God in whom I trust... He will cover you with His feathers, and under His wings you will find refuge... you will not fear the terror of the night, not the arrow that flies by day." (Psalm 91:1-2, 4-5)

Aren't you weary of letting the arrows from the enemy come in? Wouldn't it be wonderful to see those arrows bounce off the window pane? Let's give ourselves permission, shall we? Put both hands on that window sill and pull it closed. Come on, you can do it!

I'd like to close this chapter with a story from the book of Mark that sums up my heart in this matter. It is such a beautiful reminder of our frailty *and* our victory in Jesus. Take a look:

> *Then one of the crowd answered and said, "Teacher, I brought You my son, who has a mute spirit. And wherever it seizes him, it throws*

him down; he foams at the mouth, gnashes his teeth, and becomes rigid. So I spoke to Your disciples, that they should cast it out, but they could not."

He answered him and said, "O faithless generation, how long shall I be with you? How long shall I bear with you? Bring him to Me." Then they brought him to Him. And when he saw Him, immediately the spirit convulsed him, and he fell on the ground and wallowed, foaming at the mouth.

So He asked his father, "How long has this been happening to him?"

And he said, "From childhood. And often he has thrown him both into the fire and into the water to destroy him. But if You can do anything, have compassion on us and help us."

Jesus said to him, "If you can believe, all things are possible to him who believes."

Immediately the father of the child cried out and said with tears, "Lord, I believe; help my unbelief!" (Mark 9:17-24 NKJV)

"Lord, I believe; help my unbelief!"

Ladies, let this be the cry of our hearts in the face of worry! This is the kind of honest faith that lets God know we believe He is who He says He is, even though we struggle to fully trust Him sometimes.

I think the difficult part for us "worry girls" is the fact that we are not guaranteed sunshine and roses. We are not promised the health and well-being of our loved ones. We are not guaranteed we will not lose our jobs, homes, or other things of value.

That's when the enemy comes in and says, *You better start fretting over that possibility. You better start thinking of ways to prevent that trial. You better turn that over and over in your mind.* And before we know it, we are consumed with dread over things that may never happen!

May I repeat that? **Before we know it, we are consumed with dread over things that may never happen.**

My prayer is that all of us will stand strong against the lies of the evil one and that we will say "NO" the next time he offers doubt in place of God's love and care for us.

Remember, worry does not add a single hour to our lives. It cannot protect, defend, or stand against the storms of life. Only genuine prayers of faith and trust in Almighty God will lead us to the peace of mind we all desire.

Chapter Two: Thoughts to Ponder and Questions to Discuss

Have you bought into the lie that worry works? What are some of the ways you justify worry?

_____

_____

_____

_____

_____

What are the two commands from God in Isaiah 41:10? What are three things God promises to do for us in that verse?

_____

_____

_____

_____

What is the difference between worrying and problem solving? Give a few examples.

_____

_____

_____

_____

What is your biggest obstacle to closing the "worry window?"

_____

_____

_____

_____

Jesus said, *"If you can believe, all things are possible to him who believes"* *(Mark 9:23).* Does this mean everything will turn out the way we think it should? Does it mean God will settle our worries according to our desires? What is Jesus really saying?

_____

_____

_____

_____

_____

Re-read Mark 9:17-24 and ponder how the father in the story must have felt. Then, memorize his words at the end. *"Lord, I believe; help my unbelief!"* Let this be your powerful prayer the next time worry sets in.

Powerful prayer to reject the lie that worry works:

Holy God, thank You for Your truth. Thank You for opening our eyes to the lies of the enemy. Lord, help us to reject those lies right here, right now. Raise us up to stand firmly on Your Word, even when we don't fully understand what is going on around us. Help us to be like the father in the story who admitted, "I believe; help my unbelief!" And assure us, Lord, that You are in control and love us more than we could ever know. We trust You today. In Jesus' name, amen.

Chapter Two Weekly Devotions

Day One: Recognizing the Lie

Scriptures: Please read Luke 12:25-32.

What changes or solutions does worry ever bring about?

_____

_____

_____

_____

_____

If worry cannot add hours to our lives, clothes to our backs, or food to our tables, why do we continue to do it?

_____

_____

_____

_____

_____

Luke 12:28 indicates that worry is a lack of faith. Do you agree or disagree? Why?

_____

_____

_____

_____

_____

Luke 12:29-30 remind us not to have an anxious mind, but to seek first...

_____

_____

Will our needs be met if we seek the kingdom of God and His righteousness? What about our wants?

_____

_____

_____

_____

_____

_____

_____

*Copy Luke 12:32 and post it in a place where you will see it often. Let it be a sweet reminder of God's loving provision.

Day Two: **Closing the Worry Window**

Scriptures: Please read John 14:1-14.

In this passage, Jesus says, "Do not let your heart be troubled." In what ways do you let worry trouble your heart? In fact, list some of the troubles of your heart right now.

_____

_____

_____

_____

_____

How does Jesus' description of Himself—The Way, The Truth, and The Life—bring you comfort?

_____

_____

_____

_____

If Jesus said that He would do anything we ask in His name, why do some prayers seem to go unanswered? How can we better understand this passage? (See John 15:7, Matthew 21:21-22.)

_____

_____

_____

_____

Worship: Go on a prayer walk and present your requests to God in Jesus' name. Believe and do not doubt!

Day Three: **Admitting Our Unbelief**

Scriptures: Please read Hebrews 3:7-12.

Rarely in the Bible do we read that the "Holy Spirit says..." More often, it is phrased, "The Lord says..." Although the Holy Spirit *is* the Lord, I find myself sitting up a little straighter when I read the words from the Spirit:

"Today, if you will hear His voice, do not harden your hearts as in the rebellion..."

How is unbelief connected to hardening our hearts?

_____

_____

_____

_____

_____

In comparison to the Israelites in the desert, how do we sometimes display a "turning away from the Lord" in our own lives?

_____

_____

_____

_____

Hebrews 3:12 warns us against having "unbelieving hearts that lead us to depart from the Living God." How is worry a form of an unbelieving heart?

_____

_____

_____

_____

Is it difficult for you to admit unbelief? Why or why not?

_____

_____

_____

_____

_____

Write your own powerful prayer to reject the lie that worry works:

_____

_____

_____

_____

_____

_____

_____

_____

_____

_____

Takeaway from Chapter Two:

There is power in rejecting the lie
that worry works and praying,

"I believe, Lord, help my unbelief!"

Chapter Three:

Humbled Worry

I believe with all my heart that God can deliver people from every type of stronghold—including worry—and deliver them in an instant. However, I also realize that for some of us, deliverance will be a process.

Closing the worry window that has been stuck open for so long may take some time—and that's OK. Consistent, powerful prayer is one of the ways in which we will loosen the hinges and begin to close the window for good.

The subtitle of this book, *Turning Every Worry into Powerful Prayer,* makes us think of prayers that are influential, compelling, or convincing. And boy, us "worry girls" want to convince God to answer in our favor, don't we?

But what if powerful prayer was really the *humblest* form of prayer?

I am reminded of Job in the Bible, and of his unimaginable pain in the face of losing everything he had, including his children. My heart skips a beat even as I type those words because the thought of that kind of grief overwhelms me. But Job turned that devastating time into *humble prayer* and worship.

> "...another messenger came and said, 'Your sons and daughters were feasting and drinking wine at the oldest brother's house, when suddenly a mighty wind swept in from the desert and struck the four corners of the house. It collapsed on them and they are dead, and I am the only one who has escaped to tell you!' At this, Job...fell to the ground in worship and said: 'Naked I came from my mother's womb, and naked I will depart. The Lord gave and the Lord has taken away; may the Name of the Lord be praised.'"
> (Job 1:18-21)

Nothing could have prepared Job for that terrible day. After all, he hadn't planned how he was going to react in time of deep despair. But because of his *daily practice* of humbling himself before God, I believe he was able to withstand the horrible news with absolute trust in God's sovereignty.

> Because of Job's daily practice of humility,
> he was able to withstand.

My sisters, we cannot know the future. Uncertainty is part of life. Bad things happen to good people. And I know that just reading those words brings on the fretful pitter-patter of your heart. After all, we want to know that everything is going to be alright. We want that happily-ever-after.

As Christians, we are assured that eternity with the Lord is our happily-ever-after. Heaven is our hope. But if we are honest with ourselves, sometimes the hope of heaven is not enough to calm our anxiousness *now*. After all, sometimes heaven feels so far away! The hope of heaven doesn't always seem to help our present worries. And yet, the Bible encourages us to keep setting our mind on things above.

"Set your mind on things above, not on things on the earth."
(Colossians 3:2 NKJV)

So, how does setting our minds on things above help resolve our earthly problems?

I'm convinced it's all about perspective.

When worries come, and they will, we can choose to dwell on them until they block our view of God's provision, or we can hold them up to the light of God's heavenly perspective.

One example would be that of financial worry. Let's say you are faced with a major setback, such as an unexpected medical bill. Your first thoughts might be, *How will I ever pay that bill? I can barely put food on the table. I am doomed to a life of debt!* But what if you chose to take those thoughts and turn them into a new perspective? Consider God's perspective...

God will supply all my needs according to His riches in glory. (Philippians 4:19)

No good thing does He withhold from those who walk uprightly. (Psalm 84:11)

You see, in the face of every worry, there is a God perspective—a perspective that is far above our current circumstances. And I believe Job had a great understanding of that. His daily walk with God gave him the strength to withstand terrible things and still bow in complete humility and worship.

Did you know that when you go before the Lord in humble prayer, you don't even need to speak a word? You can simply go to your knees and be silent. He knows the depths of every fear. He hears the unspoken lament of your pain. He just *knows.*

"This is what the Sovereign Lord, the Holy One of Israel, says, 'In repentance and rest is your salvation, in quietness and trust is your strength." (Isaiah 30:15 NIV)

In times of intense anxiety, the last thing I want to do is be quiet before the Lord. I tend to let my mind run wild, and before I know it, I am doing everything *but* resting in Him.

"In quietness and trust is your strength…"

Job knew what it meant to fully rest in God. Before the trials came, he must have practiced daily submission to his Maker, for he was completely humble in his prayers and actions.

So, what does that look like for us? Here are some tangible ways we can daily commit to a heart of humbleness in our faith:

- **Worship often**

  Singing along with the radio station is not the only way to worship. In fact, I would venture to say we can worship without any music at all. That may sound strange coming from a musician, but as a child of God, I know, without a shadow of a doubt, that worship is far more than just singing a song.

  What leads you into deep and meaningful communion with God? It might be beautiful music or a walk outside with a view of God's creation. Maybe, it is simply opening the Word of God and meditating on a passage of truth. No matter what, incorporate worship into your daily life. Worship, and worship often.

- **Surrender everything**

There is nothing wrong with presenting our requests before the Lord and asking for His divine favor. But at the end of the day, we must be willing to say, "Not my will but Yours be done."

When we get to the place where we can honestly and sincerely speak those words, we will be practicing humble faith like Job.

Too often, we want what we want, and there is a sense of entitlement to our prayers. But let us always surrender our plans to His mighty purpose. Sweet, sweet, surrender.

- **Realize it's all His**

Our spouses, our children, and every blessing we have comes from the hand of God. We don't deserve them. We haven't earned them. They are gifts from our loving Creator. We must be willing to pry our hands away from holding everyone and everything too tightly.

You know, I remember when I first heard the song *Blessed Be Your Name* by Matt Redman. In it, he writes about God giving and taking away. Yet, in all of it, we can still say, "Blessed be Your name."

Job was the purest example of this when he said, "The Lord gave and the Lord has taken away; may the name of the Lord be praised."

Sisters, let's remind ourselves that all the good things in our lives are from the Lord, by the Lord, and for the Lord. Let's humble ourselves like Job and remember that powerful prayer doesn't necessarily mean fists raised and words shouted to the heavens. Instead, some of the most powerful prayers have been the humblest of prayers.

Chapter Three: Thoughts to Ponder and Questions to Discuss:

How would you define humility? Does that word make you think of someone who is weak? Do you personally struggle with humility?

_____

_____

_____

_____

How difficult would it be for you to praise God in the midst of a severe trial? Would it be the first or last thing on your mind?

_____

_____

_____

Ponder or discuss this statement: "Sometimes the hope of heaven is not enough to calm our anxiousness _now_." Do you agree or disagree?

_____

_____

_____

In Isaiah 30:15-16, God says that in "_____ and _____ is our salvation, and in _____ and _____ is our strength."

What picture does this verse paint for you?

_____

_____

_____

_____

Chapter Three: Weekly Devotions

Day One: Humble in the Sight of God

Scriptures: Please read Ezra 8:21-23.

Ezra had the monumental task of leading thousands of Israelites from Babylon to Jerusalem after 70 years in captivity. Imagine the hardships they faced! He proclaimed a fast at the river of Ahava for the people and their "little ones" to seek God's will. How does fasting and seeking God's will go hand-in-hand? How does fasting indicate a heart of humility before God?

_____

_____

_____

_____

Have you ever fasted? What was your experience like?

_____

_____

_____

_____

Ezra resisted going to the king for help and provision. He chose to rely fully on God. In what ways have you turned to man in times of worry instead of turning to the Lord?

_____

_____

_____

_____

_____

God answered Ezra's prayer. Because he was willing to wait for the Lord's provision, the Israelites received what they needed for the journey. Are you willing to wait on God? Or will you allow worry to interrupt your waiting?

_____

_____

_____

_____

_____

_____

_____

_____

Day Two: **Humble Surrender**

Scriptures: Please read 1 Peter 5:6-7.

Do you believe God genuinely cares about your worries? Why or why not?

_____

_____

_____

_____

_____

Is it a struggle for you to believe the Lord will "lift you up" in due time?

_____

_____

_____

_____

_____

When the Bible tells us to humble ourselves under His mighty hand, what imagery comes to mind as you picture what that means?

_____

_____

_____

_____

Day Three: **Worship Anyway**

Scriptures: Please read Job 1:20-21.

Genuine worship is one the most intimate ways we can humble ourselves in the presence of God. There is something miraculous about offering praise in the midst of hardship that brings us to a place of peace. What song immediately leads you into a place of worship and peace?

_____

_____

_____

When intense worry comes, is your first thought to panic or to praise?

_____

_____

_____

How is Job's example an inspiration to you? What parts are difficult for you to accept?

_____

_____

_____

_____

Even though Job loved his family immensely, he didn't hold on to them too tightly. Read Job 1:21 again, and copy the verse below. Even if it is difficult to accept, begin to pray this verse as a declaration that you will release your grip of worry and choose humble praise.

_____

_____

_____

_____

Write your own powerful prayer of humble praise to God:

_____

_____

_____

_____

_____

_____

_____

_____

_____

_____

_____

_____

_____

_____

_____

_____

_____

Takeaway from Chapter Three:

Powerful prayers are the humblest of prayers that say,
"Lord, no matter what, blessed be Your name!"

Chapter Four:

Thankful Worry

Our human nature, in times of stress and worry, is to freak out, complain, and be anything but thankful. After all, when something bad happens, we aren't usually in the frame of mind to stop and thank God.

However, what if thankfulness was a foundation for turning every worry into powerful prayer?

"I have learned to be content whatever the circumstances. I know what it is to be in need and I know what it is to have plenty. I have learned the secret of being content in any and every situation, whether well-fed or hungry, whether living in plenty or in want. I can do everything through him who gives me strength." (Philippians 4:11-13 NIV)

What a wealth of wisdom we are given from this passage! As Paul penned these words to the Philippians, he gave clues to the secret of being content through every trial.

- He *learned* to be content whatever the circumstance.

- He *knew* both hardship and comfort.
- He *realized* he could do everything in the strength of the Lord.

Paul knew the secret of living from a place of gratefulness and contentment because He relied on God's strength. And the secret of contentment has been made known to us as well! After all, we have the same Holy Spirit Paul had.

It may seem like saying "thank you" in times of trouble isn't an honest representation of our true feelings. But believe me, when we *choose* to thank Him through every trial, His peace will not fail to cover our circumstances (I know this from personal experience). Things might be a mess around us, but God's peace will center us.

> "Be anxious for nothing, but in everything by prayer and supplication, with thanksgiving, let your requests be made known to God; and the peace of God, which surpasses all understanding, will guard your hearts and minds through Christ Jesus." (Philippians 4:6-7 NKJV)

I love the reminder to "be anxious for nothing." When our prayers rise to the throne of God, surrounded by thanksgiving, there will be no room left for anxiety!

We may wear the carpet out by going to our knees again and again, but when we thank God in every circumstance, worry doesn't stand a chance.

> "...and the peace of God, which surpasses all understanding, will guard your hearts and minds through Christ Jesus."

Isn't peace what us "worry girls" long for most? At the end of the day, don't we just want to rest our heads on our pillows in perfect peace? Ladies, let's turn all our worries into *thankful* prayers. Let's lift our arms in praise even through tough times.

Here are a few tangible things we can do on a daily basis to cultivate a heart of thanksgiving:

- **Write down your "thanks"**

  From the warm water that comes out of the faucet, to the precious baby you hold in your arms, God's blessings can easily fill a whole page. Write down everything you are thankful for. Post your list on the fridge and add to it daily.

- **Hide the Word in your heart**

  We need the Scriptures more than bread and water. We need to be able to recall the words of God in times of trial and speak them aloud over the situation. Memorize the passages that speak clearly to your heart. Write them on index cards and tape them everywhere.

- **Remind yourself of what you know**

  In times of crisis or intense worry, we often forget what we know to be true. Do we *know* that God is sovereign? Do we *know* He sees it all? Do we *know* He hears us? We must constantly remind ourselves of what we KNOW to be true, even when we don't feel it.

Sisters, while I want nothing more than for us to have smooth sailing in life, and for the sun to shine down on everything we do, I know that this is not how life works. So, we have a choice. We can let worry rob us of joy and contentment, or we can thank God in the trials and learn to be content in all circumstances.

Chapter Four: Thoughts to Ponder and Questions to Discuss:

How quick are you to panic when trials come? Does it ever cross your mind to thank God in the midst of worry? (It's OK to be honest!)

_____

_____

_____

_____

From the list of tangible things you can do to cultivate thankfulness, which one speaks most to you? (Writing a hundred thank you's, turning on worship, memorizing Scripture, reminding yourself of what you KNOW to be true?)

_____

_____

_____

_____

How can you begin a new habit of thanking God every day—even in the face of worry?

_____

_____

_____

_____

Chapter Four: Weekly Devotions

Day One: Thank Him Anyway

Scriptures: Please read 1 Thessalonians 5:16-18.

Have you ever wondered what it really means to "pray without ceasing?" In your mind's eye, how would you describe it?

_____

_____

_____

_____

_____

Does "rejoice always" mean we should never express sorrow or sadness?

_____

_____

_____

_____

One thing we know for certain about God's will is that we are to give thanks in all circumstances. How does this reinforce your commitment to do God's will?

_____

_____

_____

_____

Day Two: **Redeeming Our Time**

Scriptures: Please read Ephesians 5:15-21.

The New King James Version of today's passage says to "walk circumspectly, redeeming the time." Look up the word *circumspectly* and write the definitions below.

_____

_____

_____

_____

So far, we've learned that worry steals precious time that we can never get back. How can we "redeem" our time? (see Ephesians 5:17)

_____

_____

_____

_____

Speaking to others in psalms, hymns, and spiritual songs may be a foreign concept to us. But what encouragements can we speak into the lives of others? Look up one or two Psalms and write down a few encouraging phrases you can share.

_____

_____

_____

_____

_____

Most Christians have been taught to pray in the name of Jesus. How important is it to give thanks in the name of Jesus? (see Ephesians 5:21)

Day Three: **Blessing God's Name**

Scriptures: Please read Psalm 100.

Serving the Lord with gladness isn't always easy. In what ways do you sometimes struggle to serve joyfully?

_____

_____

_____

_____

_____

Psalm 100: 3 reminds us that God is the One in control. He is the One who has made us and the One who leads us like a Shepherd. How is persistent worry a form of trying to take back control?

_____

_____

_____

_____

By entering into the Lord's presence with thanksgiving, we are blessing the name of the Lord. Look up at least 2 more verses that refer to blessing the Lord. Write them below.

_____

_____

_____

_____

_____

From verse 5 of Psalm 100, write down the 3 descriptions of God.

_____

_____

_____

_____

_____

Write your own powerful prayer of thanksgiving to God:

_____

_____

_____

_____

_____

_____

_____

_____

_____

_____

_____

_____

_____

Takeaway from Chapter Four:

Powerful prayers say, "Thank You, even in this, God!"

Chapter Five:

Assurance in the Face of Worry

ssurance can be described as *a guarantee, a promise, or a word of honor.* And it's human nature to want assurance that everything is going to turn out okay.

Think about it this way: We are more likely to buy products or services that are guaranteed to work. We're more likely to depend on friends who keep their promises. And, we're definitely more likely to trust someone who can prove that their word is honorable.

Am I right?

But as we all know from life experience, there are many things in this world that we are *not* assured of.

We are not assured of perfect health.

We are not assured of financial prosperity.

We are not assured of complete safety for ourselves or our loved ones.

It's these non-assurances that cause us to worry and keep us awake at night. And many of us wonder why God doesn't guarantee these good things in our lives.

What assurances *do* we have in the face of worry?

Remember the old hymn...*Blessed assurance, Jesus is mine. O what a foretaste of glory divine...*

Those words remind us of the greatest assurance we have...the blessed assurance of Jesus, our Savior and Redeemer.

As the Scriptures say,

"You will keep in perfect peace him whose mind is steadfast, because he trusts in You." (Isaiah 26:3)

I love the word *steadfast* because it speaks of reliability, dependability, and something that is unwavering. It is solid and immovable. And I don't know about you, but I want to be solid and immovable in my faith.

One of the most remarkable stories I've ever read is that of Martin and Gracia Burnham. Perhaps you've heard of them. For one whole year they were taken captive in the Philippine jungle by radical terrorists. Without proper food, shelter, or clothing, they faced unimaginable hardship. Their story is riveting! But it's also terrifying and heart-wrenching.

As I read Gracia's book, *In the Presence of My Enemies*, I find myself questioning how the Lord they loved allowed them to go through such a long and horrible ordeal. In my mind, I want the assurance that God will prevent such terrible things from happening. Yet, I know that His ways are not my ways and His thoughts are not my thoughts (Isaiah 55: 8-9).

Through the Burnham's unthinkable trial, an incredible testimony of steadfastness was born—a steadfastness of utter dependency on a holy God, no matter what.

This is, perhaps, the most difficult aspect of turning our worries into powerful prayers. For it includes a deep trust that says, "No matter what, Lord, You are sovereign."

"I know who I have believed, that He is able to guard what I have entrusted to Him for that day." (2 Timothy 1:12)

Sisters, do we know *Whom* we have believed? Do we trust that He is able to guard what we've committed to Him? Can we somehow look past the current whirlwind of turmoil we are facing and actually trust Him?

"Because the Sovereign Lord helps me, I will not be disgraced. Therefore I have set my face like flint, and I know I will not be put to shame. He who vindicates me is near."
(Isaiah 50:7-8)

He who vindicates us is near. We must determine to set our faces like flint (like stone) toward the One who gives us divine assurance in the midst of trials.

Please don't misunderstand and think I am asking you to deal with adversity emotionlessly or without feeling. We were designed with intense feelings and emotions. And when the tough times come, we should address our emotions honestly.

My tendency has always been to square my shoulders and bear things stoically. I'm not one to cry easily or wear my emotions on my sleeve, so to say. But sisters, we were created to laugh, cry, and even get angry.

I have a good friend who is a "crier." She tears up easily, and before we know it, she's crying again. I tease her about it, but in all honesty, I wish I was as authentic with my own emotions. After all, we can display deep emotion and still rest assured that God is in control —that He loves us more than we can comprehend.

So, what can we be absolutely sure of in this life? Here are a few truths to read and ponder as we close this chapter. My prayer for you is that you will commit to memory one or all of these verses. You will definitely need them along the way.

"The work of righteousness will be peace, and the effect of righteousness, quietness and assurance forever." (Isaiah 32:17)

"For You have been a shelter for me, a strong tower from the enemy. I will abide in Your tabernacle forever; I will trust in the shelter of Your wings." (Psalm 61:3-4)

"As you, therefore, have received Christ Jesus the Lord, so walk in Him, rooted and built up in Him and established in the faith, as you have been taught, abounding in it with thanksgiving." (Colossians 2:6-7)

Be assured today, sisters. Even in your worry, you can know that God is unchangeable, unshakable, and unwavering. He's got you. He's got this.

Chapter Five: Thoughts to Ponder and Questions to Discuss:

What does "blessed assurance" mean to you?

_____

_____

_____

_____

_____

How difficult is it for you to believe, that no matter what, God is sovereign?

_____

_____

_____

_____

After hearing about the Burnham's story of survival in the Philippine jungle, how do you view such hardship in light of God's love? Does the fear of severe trial cause you to worry unnecessarily?

_____

_____

_____

_____

From Isaiah 26: 3, and 2 Timothy 1:12, what assurances do we have?

_____

_____

_____

_____

What 3 promises can you immediately recall from the Bible? Find them in the Scriptures and write them below.

_____

_____

_____

_____

_____

_____

Chapter Five: Weekly Devotions

Day One: Overcome

Scriptures: Please read John 16:33.

What does "being of good cheer" actually mean for everyday life?

_____

_____

_____

_____

_____

What does it mean to you that Christ has overcome the world?

_____

_____

_____

_____

_____

Write an acrostic poem for the word O-V-E-R-C-O-M-E. (Simply write a word or phrase next to each letter that describes what it means to overcome.)

O

V

E

R

C

O

M

E

Day Two: **Do Not Be Dismayed**

Scriptures: Please read Joshua 1:8-9.

Multiple times in the first chapter of Joshua, the Lord says, *"Be strong and courageous. Do not be afraid."* I believe God repeated that phrase over and over because He knew exactly what Joshua would face. God knows everything we are going through and everything we *will* go through. His constant reminder is to be strong and courageous. From Joshua 1:8, what do we know to be the source of our strength?

_____

_____

_____

Honestly, do you view the Bible as a source of strength and comfort? Why or why not?

_____

_____

_____

_____

When worry comes, make it a habit to go to the Word first. Before you try to solve the problem on your own, or turn to others for help, go to the Bible and meditate upon the life-giving words. Today, choose a Psalm to turn to in times of worry. Which Psalm will you read the next time you are afraid?

_____

_____

_____

_____

Day Three: **You Do Not Need to Fight**

Scriptures: Please read 2 Chronicles 20:13-18.

As all of Judah stood before the Lord—men, women, and children—God comforted them with these phrases:

"Do not be afraid or dismayed because of this great multitude."

"The battle is not yours, but God's."

"You will not need to fight in this battle."

"Stand still and see the salvation of the Lord who is with you."

Which of those phrase comforts your heart the most? Why?

_____

_____

_____

_____

_____

After the people heard those comforting words from the Lord, what did they do?

_____

_____

_____

_____

_____

Perhaps, the most powerful verse from 2 Chronicles 20 is verse 17: "You will not need to fight in this battle. Position yourselves, stand still and see the salvation of the Lord, who is with you..."

Reread those comforting words from the Lord. Really internalize them. "You will not need to fight the battle. Only position yourself, stand still, and see the salvation of the Lord. He is with you."

What do those words mean for you, personally?

_____

_____

_____

_____

Worship: Go to your prayer closet and stand still before the Lord. No matter what worries are weighing you down, be still and know that He is with you.

Write your own powerful prayer of God's assurance in the face of worry:

_____

_____

_____

_____

_____

_____

Takeaway from Chapter Five:

Powerful prayers come from the assurance of God's presence in the face of worry.

Chapter Six:
Genuine Worry

I can't assume to know what worries you most, but if I had to guess, I would say that the well-being of your loved ones is probably at the top of your list.

For me, the hours, days, and weeks that I've worried over my family's safety would probably add up to years of my life. And now that I have grandchildren, I find myself with even more precious people to worry about!

But sisters, the Lord never intended for us to grasp our loved ones so tightly. There's no way we can hold them as close as He holds them. God loves and cares for our families far more than we could ever love and care for them.

Many years ago, when my daughter was still a toddler, we found out we were going to have another baby. With our oldest boys so close together, I was looking forward to having a baby who would be close to our daughter's age. But sadly, before the 1st trimester was over, I miscarried.

I was given a few books by some well-meaning friends. And in one of them, I read about angels guarding my baby until one day, I would get to hold them in heaven. But for some reason, I had a hard time grasping that thought.

Now, I'm ashamed to admit this, but I remember thinking that *I* was the best one to take care of my baby—even more than the angels in heaven and even more than God. After much emotional struggle over this, and lots of prayer, it became a turning point for me to realize that God's tender love far outweighed anything I could *ever* give my children.

It was through that difficult time that I was convicted I must place my loved ones fully into the Lord's hands. It wasn't easy for me. It still isn't. I sometimes find myself so afraid of what *might* happen that I miss out on the beauty that is happening right now.

Can I repeat that?

> I sometimes find myself so afraid of what might happen, I miss out on the beauty that is happening right now.

One of my favorite authors, Lysa TerKeurst, shares her beautiful insight in an article called, "A Mom's Greatest Fear."

I especially relate to her when she says, *"Yes, I ask for them to be kept safe. Yes, I believe in the power and provision of prayer. But, I have to realize that I cannot control my children's safety. Not by my prayers, not by my worries, and certainly not by my fears."*

Sisters, what Lisa says is true. We cannot control the wellbeing of our loved ones a hundred percent of the time. The only thing we can control is how we will handle our worries. We get to *choose* what to do with every worry that comes along.

(https://lysaterkeurst.com/wp-content/uploads/pdf/A_Moms_Greatest_Fear.pdf)

When worries come about the health and well-being of our loved ones, we can let those worries pull us under, leaving us captivated by fear, or we can remind ourselves that God is the gentle Healer. He is the loving Father. He loves those whom we love far greater than we ever could.

God loves those we love far greater than we ever could.

Apart from the well-being of those we love, another genuine worry is the one covered in dollar signs. The stress of not having enough money can be overwhelming. Constant questions about provision circle around our minds until we are completely worn out. Questions like...

- How will I buy groceries?
- How will I pay for that unexpected car repair?
- How will I pay off that medical bill?
- How will I be able to buy what my kids need?

These are very real concerns. However, we have a God who truly does provide for our needs according to His riches in glory. (See Philippians 4:19.)

It was over twenty years ago that my husband and I took the plunge and purchased our first home. I remember calling my parents the night before we closed the deal; I was crying because I was scared to death. Our rent payment of $375 per month was going to jump to a $750 house payment! I was so worried I felt sick.

Those were hard years financially. I even fretted over how we were going to buy winter coats and school clothes for the kids. But in that season of genuine worry, the Lord cultivated something in me that I could never have developed on my own. He taught me a level of trust I didn't have before. Time and again He came through with exactly what we needed and more.

I feel very humbled thinking back to that time. I actually appreciate those experiences, because they taught me things like the value of clipping coupons, ordering water instead of soda at restaurants, and driving our old cars until they couldn't run anymore. Even in easier financial times, I've still tried to be frugal, and it's all because of those tough, learning years.

What about you? Are you struggling to trust God with your finances?

If so, my heart goes out to you. The everyday stuff of life certainly does challenge us, and it can seem unrelenting. If we are completely honest, sometimes it feels like we can trust God to the moon and back, but at the end of the day, the bills still need to be paid.

> Sometimes it feels like we can trust God to the moon and back, but at the end of the day, the bills still need to be paid.

So, what can we do? We can start by taking Jesus' words seriously. In Matthew 6:25-33, He says,

> "Therefore I say to you, do not worry about your life, what you will eat or what you will drink; nor about your body, what you will put on. Is not life more than food and the body more than clothing? Look at the birds of the air, for they neither sow nor reap nor gather into barns; yet your heavenly Father feeds them. Are you not of more value than they? Which of you by worrying can add one cubit to his stature? So why do you worry about clothing? Consider the lilies of the field, how they grow: they neither toil nor spin; and yet I say to you that even Solomon in all his glory was not arrayed like one of these. Now if God so clothes the grass of the field, which today is, and tomorrow is thrown into the oven, will He not much more clothe you, O you of little faith? Therefore do not worry, saying, 'What shall we eat?' or 'What shall we drink?' or 'What shall we wear?' For after all these things the Gentiles seek. For your heavenly Father knows that you need all these things. But seek first the kingdom of God and His righteousness, and all these things shall be added to you. Therefore do not worry about tomorrow, for tomorrow will worry about its own things. Sufficient for the day is its own trouble."

Sisters, the birds do not sow or reap or store away in barns, yet our heavenly Father feeds them. I love that! In fact, it is summertime as I write this, and the birds are my alarm clock in the morning. Sharply at 4:20 a.m., they begin their loud chirping. I imagine the baby birds crying for food as their parents frantically look for worms. But the thing is, they eventually get fed!

So let me ask you a question: Are you afraid to *ask* God for what you need?

He knows it already! He longs to give you the desire of your heart. It's just that our hearts don't always coincide with His perfect will. At the end of the day, we must always surrender our will to His. *But we shouldn't be afraid to ask.*

Honestly, I try to lay everything out before God—my thoughts, plans, needs, wants and ramblings. I point out the broken faucet, the airline ticket that needs to be purchased, and even the running shoes I would like to have. But I always, *always* know that the shoes might have to wait in order for the faucet to be fixed; that I may have to drive instead of fly. Or I might simply have to do without. I truly want God's will above my own. And because of that, I feel free to ask for His help and blessing.

Ladies, genuine worries will come. But let's be women who take those concerns straight to the throne of God. Let's loosen our grip on our loved ones and on our financial needs. Our God, Jehovah-Jireh, truly is our Provider. His very name assures us that He will supply all of our needs. Praise be to the God who provides!

Chapter Six: Thoughts to Ponder and Questions to Discuss

What are your top 3 genuine worries?

_____

_____

_____

_____

_____

How does persistent worry affect your sleep? How many times per week does worry keep you awake at night? Read Psalm 4:7-8. Make that your bedtime Scripture passage.

_____

_____

_____

_____

_____

_____

What promises from God can you recall when you are worried about the well-being and safety of your loved ones? (List 2-3 promises from the Scriptures.)

_____

_____

_____

_____

_____

When it comes to financial worry, how sure are you that God will provide? Do you have an example of how He provided for you in the past?

_____

_____

_____

_____

_____

What things could you do *without* to make your financial burden a little easier? (Be honest!)

_____

_____

_____

_____

How easy is it for you to ask God for the things you need or want? What is the best way to ask?

_____

_____

_____

_____

Chapter Six: Weekly Devotions

Day One: Effective, Fervent Prayer

Scriptures: Please read James 5:13-18.

The passage in James tells us exactly what to do when we are worried about the health and well-being of our loved ones. List the actions we are to take from James 5:13-18.

_____

_____

_____

_____

The Bible says that the effective, fervent prayer of a righteous man avails much. What makes prayer effective? What does fervent prayer look like? What makes a man righteous? (See Matthew 6:9-13, 1 Samuel 1:9-18, Philippians 3:8-9.)

_____

_____

_____

_____

Day Two: **The Benefits of Trial**

Scriptures: Please read Romans 5:1-4.

The first verse in Romans 5 gives us one reason we have peace. What is that reason?

_____

_____

_____

Justified means that we have been made righteous in the sight of God. From Whom does our righteousness come?

_____

_____

_____

_____

There is always a greater purpose that goes beyond our genuine worries. From Romans 5:3, what are the benefits of going through trials?

_____

_____

_____

_____

Worship: Be creative by drawing or painting a picture of "peace." What colors will you choose? What pictures come to mind when you think of "peace?"

Day Three: **I Shall Not Want**

Scriptures: Please read Psalm 23.

In this familiar passage of Scripture, David starts out by saying, "The Lord is my Shepherd. I shall not want." How does this ring true in your heart regarding your financial worries?

_____

_____

_____

_____

In Psalm 23:2-3, David uses 3 beautiful imageries—green pastures, still waters, and paths of righteousness. Think of a few more peaceful scenes from God's creation that bring calmness to your soul.

_____

_____

_____

_____

Verses 5 and 6 of Psalm 23 speak of abundance. When we worry about money, it's easy to forget about God's abundance. Write down the abundant ways God provided for David. Then, write 2-3 ways the Lord has blessed you.

_____

_____

_____

_____

Worship: Rewrite the 23rd Psalm in your own handwriting. Keep it in your Bible or wallet as a reminder of God's loving faithfulness.

Your Own Powerful Prayer in the Face of Genuine Worry...

_____

_____

_____

_____

_____

_____

_____

_____

_____

_____

_____

_____

_____

_____

_____

_____

_____

_____

Takeaway from Chapter Six:

Genuine worries will come, but there is power in *asking* God to handle them!

Chapter Seven:

Worrying about the Hard Stuff

I put this chapter toward the end because it's not one I feel totally comfortable writing. It has to do with the hard stuff of life. For as much as we'd like to believe that everyone and everything will be ok during our time on earth, that's not the way it always works.

As an idealistic girl, happy endings are the things I like to imagine. I want to believe the world can be a happy-go-lucky place where everyone drinks an ice-cold Coke and sings in a meadow (remember that 70s commercial?). But real life tells me something different.

A few years ago, I heard about a young wife and mom in my own community who passed away from breast cancer. She wrote about her journey in a very candid and beautiful eBook, The Hardest Peace: Expecting Grace in the Midst of Life's Hard. (Tippetts, Kara (2014-10-01). The Hardest Peace: Expecting Grace in the Midst of Life's Hard (p. 130). David C. Cook. Kindle Edition.)

This particular section of her book moved me deeply:

"If I really sit and listen to God, He will lift the dread. The dread and fear are what so often steal our peace and leave us on the edges of our moments exhausted. We meet the scary of life and forget to

turn to God and listen and know His peace. We scramble to control, fix, and protect from hard. The imagined fears and worries often break us more than reality."

Kara's sentence, *"If I really sit and listen to God, He will lift the dread,"* is an amazing reminder for us. For in the midst of terminal cancer and navigating herself through it, Kara discovered the key to peace.

If we really LISTEN, God will bring peace.

Do you believe that today?

Perhaps, in our instant gratification culture, we've lost our ability to stop and wait on God. Maybe, we are too busy asking Him for things and not taking time to listen—*really* listen.

In the noise of everything around us, we struggle to hear God's voice. His comforts are crowded out by the buzz of the world. So, how can we combat this? How can we turn to the voice of the Lord in the sea of voices around us?

Sisters, we can rise above the noise and declare the very words of God!

The most powerful prayers we can pray are straight from the Scriptures. To read a Proverb or Psalm, as a prayer to the Lord, is the quickest way to bring the peace we long for.

> "By day the Lord directs his love, at night His song is with me— a prayer to the God of my life." (Psalm 42:8)

What prayer to the God of your life do you long to speak? Are the words eluding you? Go to His word and begin pouring out your soul to Him. The words will be like honey to your lips and joy to your soul. Truly, the worry and dread will be removed.

"Establish Your word to Your servant, who is devoted to fearing You. Turn away my reproach which I dread, for Your judgments are good. Behold, I long for Your precepts. Revive me in Your righteousness."
(Psalm 119:38-40)

The Word of God is powerful in our sorrows. His precepts, which are the ordinances that direct our lives, are perfect and holy. Revival comes in Him alone. Worry is banished in Him alone.

I recently read a blog called Choose Your Hard from author and speaker Stasi Eldredge. She wrote:

> "Sometimes, it's hard to pray. It's hard to find the time. It's hard to live your day with strength, hope, and integrity if you don't. It's hard to pursue Living Water. It's hard to live in a dry and thirsty land without it. Choose your hard." (https://wildatheart.org/blogs/stasi/choose-your-hard)

Choosing the difficult thing—the right thing—in the middle of worry is a decision only we can make. We can hear bad news and crumble, or we can take it to that quiet place and cry out to the God who hears.

I don't like hard stuff. No one does. I like easy-peasy. But here we are living in a world that has been decaying around us since the first bite that Eve took of the forbidden fruit. Things aren't going to get better. The Bible is clear about the end.

But God...God in His faithfulness, *brand-spanking new every morning*, takes the hard and makes it bearable. He takes the fear and douses it with perfect love. And He takes the worry and says, "I've got this, Daughter. I've got you."

I've got this, Daughter. I've got you.

What is the *hard* in your life today? What difficult thing are you facing? Please stop the turning of your mind and listen. Really listen. He has a word for you—words of comfort and perfect peace. Choose a passage from the Bible and pray it. Pray it loud and pray it clear. Then, as the Lord surrounds you, as he removes your dread, lift up a hand of praise to Him.

Chapter Seven: Thoughts to Ponder and Questions to Discuss:

Are you the kind of person who likes to believe in happy endings? Or are you more of a realistic thinker?

_____

_____

_____

_____

_____

When the hard stuff comes, does it hinder your faith in a good and loving God?

_____

_____

_____

_____

_____

What phrase from Kara's journey with cancer spoke most to your heart?

_____

_____

_____

_____

_____

Choose a Psalm this week to pray aloud. Write a few comforting phrases from that Psalm.

_____

_____

_____

_____

Chapter Seven: Weekly Devotions

Day One: Wisdom Over Worry

Scriptures: Please read Proverbs 2: 1-9.

This chapter of Proverbs gives us a beautiful list of actions. Fill in the rest of the phrases below. (I am writing from the NKJV.)

receive _____

treasure _____

incline _____

apply _____

cry out _____

lift up _____

What happens when we seek wisdom as a hidden treasure? (verses 4 & 5)

_____

_____

_____

_____

In verses 7 & 8, what protective things does God do for the upright?

_____

_____

_____

_____

Day Two: **Hard Places and God's Comfort**

Scriptures: Please read Psalm 42:5-8.

Is your soul downcast today? What is one answer from Psalm 42:5 for feeling downcast?

_____

_____

_____

In what hard place was the writer of this Psalm? (See verses 3, 7, and 9.)

_____

_____

_____

According to verse 8, what comforts does God give in the daytime and nighttime?

_____

_____

_____

Worship: Take a large sheet of paper and write the words, "Put your hope in God!" Tape it in a prominent place as a reminder of where your hope lies.

Day Three: New EVERY Morning

Scriptures: Please read Lamentations 3:1-24.

Is it difficult to understand why the Lord would allow Jeremiah to go through such an oppressive and lonely time? Write your honest thoughts and pray for wisdom.

_____

_____

_____

_____

_____

How does Lamentations 3:21-24 fill your heart with hope and comfort?

_____

_____

_____

_____

_____

Write Lamentations 3:22-24 here:

_____

_____

_____

_____

_____

Worship: Listen to the old song "Great Is Thy Faithfulness" on YouTube or another platform. What is your favorite line?

Write your own powerful prayer for the hard stuff of life...

_____

_____

_____

_____

_____

_____

_____

_____

_____

_____

_____

_____

_____

_____

_____

_____

_____

_____

_____

_____

_____

Takeaway from Chapter Seven:

Declaring God's faithfulness is a
powerful prayer in difficult times.

Chapter Eight:

Future Worries

O n any given day, at any given time, we can read the news headlines and shudder. Whether it be that we have more technology capturing every bad thing in the world, or that things are truly getting worse, it's scary, don't you think?

Many of us feel like we can endure a lot of things, (and have endured a lot of things), but what about our children and grandchildren? What will they have to go through as time goes on? How will they survive the ever-growing darkness in the culture?

In one of my recent blogs, I shared a personal story about surviving in a very scary world. Here is an excerpt:

I watch my tiny grandsons playing with cars, digging in the dirt (eating the dirt), and laughing with dimpled smiles...

And I worry.

How will they survive in a place where people randomly shoot other people, where everyone does what "feels" right, and where nuclear deals are being made with the bad guys?

I won't always be there to protect them. And even if I was, could I?

We teach our children to play nice, eat their vegetables, and wash their hands—and rightfully so. But what about knowing God, loving God, and loving others?

Perhaps we should be honest with them and tell them we don't understand all the injustices in the world or how to right the wrongs, but that God is still sovereign.

Maybe we should teach them that really loving someone means telling them hard things—things they don't want to hear, but telling them anyway. Above all else, we should let them know that there will be a day when their own hearts will need to decide whether Jesus is Who He says He is, or not. And that their final decision will lead to their final destination.

Sisters, the future doesn't need to be a source of worry when we already know how it ends. It's like reading a story that's full of peril and danger, only to turn the page and see that they really did live happily ever after.

> It's like reading a story that is full of peril and danger, only to turn the page and see that they really did live happily ever after.

Remember the popular books from the 80s and 90s where you could choose your own adventure? You'd get to a certain point and then be given choices to keep reading or flip to another page. Depending on your decision, the story would have a different outcome. (And if you were like me, you read all the different endings and picked the one you liked best.)

As believers in Christ, we've already chosen the very best ending possible! There is no "skip-to-page-eleven." The story is written! We chose the perfect ending to life's adventure the minute we accepted Jesus as our Lord and Savior.

Here is our happily-ever-after recorded in the book of Revelation...

"Then the angel showed me the river of the water of life, as clear as crystal, flowing from the throne of God and of the Lamb down the middle of the great street of the city. On each side of the river stood the tree of life, bearing twelve crops of fruit, yielding its fruit every month. And the leaves of the tree are for the healing of the nations. No longer will there be any curse. The throne of God and of the Lamb will be in the city, and His servants will serve Him. They will see His face, and His name will be on their fore-heads. There will be no more night. They will not need the light of a lamp or the light of the sun, for the Lord God will give them light. And they will reign forever and ever." (Revelation 22:1-5 NIV)

I don't know about you, but I could read this passage a hundred times and still get goosebumps and break into a huge smile! The end is written and *we are included* in the story. We will serve the Living God, see His face, and bear His name forever and ever.

Worries about the future have no merit. While it's true that we cannot know exactly what will happen from day to day, we can equip ourselves with Scriptures to rely on in the day of trouble. Even a few sentences from God's Word can diminish the intensity of worry.

Personally, I have a few favorite phrases from the Bible—simple, one-line sentences that cause my heart to leap for joy because they are a summary of my hope in God. Any time I feel myself getting anxious, I only have to remind myself of these words and the peace of God washes over me. I hope that by sharing them with you, you will be able to claim them in times of trouble as well.

- **In the beginning…God**

  When I speak these four words, the very first words of the Bible, there is power in knowing that He was there in the beginning. And you know what? He is here now. And He will be there in the future, for all eternity. In the beginning…God.

- **It is finished.**

  Every single time I remember the words of Jesus—His final words on earth—I want to raise my hands in victory. As He spoke the words, "It is finished," the veil of the temple was torn in two, allowing us to enter the most holy place. Sin and death are overcome in the finished work of Jesus Christ on the cross. These are powerful, beautiful words to remember in the face of adversity.

- **He is risen!**

  I don't wait until Easter Sunday to shout this with joy. These 3 little words remind us that we are victorious over sin and death! Hooray! The fact that Jesus died yet rose again is the best possible news we could ever receive. When we feel worries crowding in, we can burst out of their grip with the best news in the universe… He is risen!

- **"I am coming quickly."**

  There is no doubt that Jesus is indeed coming soon. Our hope rests in that very fact. And no matter what we are enduring here, no matter what the news headlines say, Jesus is coming back! Sisters, when today feels too hard, and the worries of life are clouding your joy, simply remind yourself that Jesus is coming quickly.

As we close the final door on worry and the hold it has on our lives, it is my sincere prayer that all of us will be able to turn every single worry into powerful prayer. I want you to be empowered to shut that window and keep it locked. Here are a few reminders of what we've learned:

- We've determined that worry does not work, and we've resisted the lie that if only we would worry enough, things would get better.

- We learned that humble prayers are often the most powerful prayers.

- We talked about thanking God, yes thanking Him, in the midst of every doubt, fear, and anxiety.

- We were encouraged to trust the Lord, no matter our circumstances. And by doing that, we learned to release the power that worry has over us.

- We were urged to pray the Word of God over every circumstance. When we don't have the words to cry out, we speak the inspired and holy words of God. And when we do, His peace washes over us.

Dear sisters, there are very real and genuine worries in life. We all have them. But in each and every worry—past, present, or future—we know how the story ends. We know that God is able to take what we've committed to Him and guard it until the day we see Him face to face. Amen!

From Psalm 24:5-10, we close our time together. We close the worry window. And we turn every worry into powerful prayer.

"They will receive blessing from the Lord and vindication from God their Savior. Such is the generation of those who seek Him, who seek your face, God of Jacob. Lift up your heads, you gates; be lifted up, you ancient doors, that the King of glory may come in. Who is this King of glory? The Lord strong and mighty, the Lord mighty in battle. Lift up your heads, you gates; lift them up, you ancient doors, that the King of glory may come in. Who is he, this King of glory? The Lord Almighty—he is the King of glory."
(Psalm 24:5-10)

Chapter Eight: Thoughts to Ponder and Questions to Discuss:

How do the news headlines or current events make you feel? Do you guard your mind from some of it? What Good News in Christ overshadows every piece of bad news that you hear?

_____

_____

_____

_____

_____

What's the most important thing to remember when we worry about future generations?

_____

_____

_____

_____

What are some Scriptural truths you can claim in times of worry?

_____

_____

_____

_____

What is your favorite part about Revelation 22:1-5?

_____

_____

_____

_____

Chapter Eight: Weekly Devotions

Day One: Power and Glory

Scriptures: Please read Matthew 24:29-31.

What amazing events in heaven and on earth will take place before Jesus returns?

_____

_____

_____

_____

_____

Why do you suppose all the tribes of the earth will mourn when they see Jesus coming in the clouds?

_____

_____

_____

_____

As worries of this life come and go, what is one thing you can remember about Jesus' glorious return?

_____

_____

_____

_____

_____

Powerful Prayer for Today: *Lord, how we long for Your return! We cannot imagine Your magnificent glory, but we long to see it. Please, Lord, do not delay. Come quickly, our God and our Redeemer. When things are tough, please remind us that there really is a happy ending. You, O God, are our happy ending. We love You and praise You...in Jesus' name.*

Worship: In your personal journal, sketch a picture of Jesus' return. Don't worry about your art skills. Just allow yourself to imagine that glorious day and draw what you hope to see.

Day Two: **Transforming Our Lowly Bodies**

Scriptures: Please read Philippians 3:20-21.

Sisters, our citizenship does not belong here. Where is our eternal home?

_____

_____

_____

How easy is it to lose sight of heaven?

_____

_____

_____

What will happen to our bodies when Jesus returns?

_____

_____

_____

_____

Verse 21 of Philippians 3 says, "Jesus will subdue all things to Himself." This indicates that all things will be brought under His authority. Can we trust Him to bring all of our worries under His authority today?

_____

_____

_____

Worship: Spend time in your prayer closet, away from all the noise and distractions. Pray for God to prepare your heart and mind for Jesus' return. Thank Him for the great expectation of our Savior's coming.

Day Three: **First and Last**

Scriptures: Please read Revelation 22:12-17.

What kind of reward do you imagine Jesus is talking about in Revelation 22:12?

_____

_____

_____

After a lifetime of worry, can you imagine the freedom you will feel when you meet Jesus face to face? What will be the first thing you say to Him?

_____

_____

_____

_____

Knowing that Jesus is the Alpha and Omega, the Beginning and the End, how does that comfort you today?

_____

_____

_____

_____

What beautiful invitation are we given in Revelation 22:17?

_____

_____

_____

_____

How can we partake of the Living Water now? How can we thirst no more, but drink of the Well that never runs dry? Write your thoughts below.

Powerful prayer for today: *Almighty God, as we close this study, we rejoice in the hope of our salvation—Jesus Christ. We know, Lord, that You are everlasting. You go before us and behind us. Thank You! Once again, we entrust each and every worry of this life to You. We are assured by Your grace and Your love that You've got this. We are so grateful. In Jesus' name, amen.*

Write your own powerful prayer for the future:

Takeaway from Chapter Eight:

Looking forward to eternity with Christ is a powerful prayer over all worries—past, present, and future.

Jennifer Waddle is an author and speaker for Christian women who feel stuck in faith and life. She is also a regular contributor for LifeWay, Crosswalk, Abide, and Christians Care International. Jennifer's online ministry is EncouragementMama.com where you can find her books and sign up for her weekly post, *Discouragement Doesn't Win*. She resides with her family near the foothills of the Rocky Mountains—her favorite place on earth.

*Your honest review of this book will help me reach more people. So please take a minute to leave a review on Amazon. Thank you so much! (If you received a free copy of this book, please state in your Amazon review that you received a free copy in exchange for an honest review.)

References and Resources
for the Journey

Does God Hear My Prayers?
https://www.gotquestions.org/does-God-hear-my-prayers.html

12 Things to Thank God for in the Midst of Affliction
www.biblestudytools.com/blogs/mark-altrogge/12-things-to-thank-god-for-in-the-midst-of-affliction.html

What Are the Promises of God? www.gotquestions.org/promises-of-God.html

Choose Your Hard, Stasi Eldridge: http://ransomedheart.com/blogs/stasi/choose-your-hard

Having a Mary Heart in a Martha World:
https://www.amazon.com/Having-Mary-Heart-Martha-World-ebook/dp/B000SEHC18/ref=sr_1_1?s=books&ie=UTF8&qid=1428593701&sr=1-1&keywords=having+a+mary+heart+in+a+martha+world)

A Mom's Greatest Fear: lysaterkeurst.com/wp-content/uploads/pdf/A_Moms_Greatest_Fear.pdf

The Hardest Peace: https://www.amazon.com/Hardest-Peace-Expecting-Grace-Midst/dp/0781412153/ref=tmm_pap_swatch_0?_encoding=UTF8&qid=&sr=

Made in the USA
Columbia, SC
02 April 2024

33916858R00059